LEADER'S GUIDE

FOR

Siddur Mah Tov
A Family Shabbat Prayer Book

How to create great worship services that reflect your community's values

A GUIDE FOR EDUCATORS, CLERGY, AND LAY LEADERS

By Rabbi Lauren Kurland and Julie Schwartz Wohl

EDITORIAL CONSULTANTS:

Rabbi Kenneth Carr

Rabbi Martin S. Cohen

Behrman House, Inc.
www.behrmanhouse.com

Contents

Introduction 4
　The Powerful Potential of Family Services 4
　Who Should Use This Guide? 4
　How to Use This Guide 4

Part One—Family Services: From Vision to Implementation 5
　🕊 **Before You Begin: Forming a Family Services Leadership Team** 5
　🕊 **Phase 1: Self-Reflection and Information Gathering** 6
　　Meeting #1: The Goals of Family Services 6
　　　Chair's Agenda 6
　　　Text Study: Why Do We Join Together as a Prayer Community? 9
　　　Identifying Priorities 10
　　　Informational Survey 11
　　　State of Our Family Services 13
　🕊 **Phase 2: Writing a Vision Statement for Family Services** 15
　　Meeting #2: Writing a Family Services Vision Statement 15
　　　Chair's Agenda 15
　　　Text Study: For the Sake of the Community 17
　　　Sample Vision Statements 18
　　Meeting #3: Expanding Our Vision 19
　　　Chair's Agenda 19
　　　Text Study: Working Together 21
　　　Expanding Our Vision Statement Worksheet 22
　　　Sample Expanded Vision Statements 23
　🕊 **Phase 3: Implementing Our Family Service** 26

Part Two—For the Service Leader: Enriching Your Services 27
General Planning Tips for Service Leaders 28
Room Setup 28
Welcoming Families 29
Building the Prayer Service 29
　　Modeh/Modah Ani 29
　　Mah Tovu 29
　　Hinei Mah-Tov 30

Birchot Hashachar	31
Psalm 150	31
V'nomar Lefanav and Hal'lu-Hodu LaShem (Conservative)	32
Bar'chu	33
Yotzeir Or	33
Ahavah Rabah	34
Sh'ma	34
V'ahavta	35
Mi Chamochah	36
Amidah	37
Oseh Shalom	38
Torah Service	38
Aleinu	40
Mourner's Kaddish	41
Adon Olam	41
Kiddush and Hamotzi	42

How to Make the Most Out of Kiddush . . . 42

Troubleshooting . . . 42

Appendix . . . 44
- Suggested Outline of the Shabbat Morning Service for Tots (3 and Younger) . . . 45
- Suggested Outline of the Shabbat Morning Service for Children Ages 4–8 . . . 46

BOOK AND COVER DESIGN ❧ Stacey May
PROJECT EDITOR ❧ Terry S. Kaye

Copyright © 2010 Behrman House, Inc.
Springfield, New Jersey
www.behrmanhouse.com
ISBN: 978-0-87441-857-6
Manufactured in the United States of America

Introduction

☙ The Powerful Potential of Family Services

On Shabbat, communities gather together to pray and study—and also to connect and socialize. Many congregations offer family services* to increase families' access to the joyful celebration of Shabbat. Family services present a valuable opportunity to bring parents and children together in Jewish prayer and tradition.

Strong family services are thoughtfully constructed to reflect congregational values and encourage both parent and child participation. This guide is designed to help you think critically about the purpose and goals of your family services, to help you implement a process for creating or enriching family services, and to give you concrete ideas that will add depth and breadth to your family service.

☙ Who Should Use This Guide?

The guide is designed for a team of professional synagogue staff working with lay leaders. The professional staff may include the rabbi, cantor, education director, worship service leader, or ritual director. Lay leaders may include ritual committee members, parents, and other volunteers.

The guide provides options for congregations currently holding family services, as well as for congregations designing a family service for the first time.

☙ How to Use This Guide

The guide consists of two complementary, yet independent, sections. You can read both sections or focus on the section most appropriate for your situation.

Section 1

Helps you develop your congregation's vision for family services by:
- Offering tips for creating a Shabbat family services leadership team
- Providing meeting outlines, sample agendas, and materials needed
- Presenting relevant Jewish texts to facilitate group discussion

Section 2

Offers practical suggestions to make services more dynamic and interactive with:
- General tips for service leaders
- A brief summary of each Shabbat morning prayer's content or context
- Specific ideas for each prayer that involve art, movement, discussion, stories, or props
- A list of prayers commonly included in family services

Throughout the process, remember that not all ideas will be right for your community or for your community right *now*. Be willing to experiment, and also be patient with the pace of change.

---

* While the term "family service" is used in this guide, your community might use another term, such as Tot Shabbat, Mini-Minyan, children's services, or junior congregation.

Part One

Family Services
From Vision to Implementation

☙ Before You Begin: Forming a Family Services Leadership Team

The first step in the process of strengthening family services is to create a Family Services Leadership Team that will guide the community's conversations about family services.

The Leadership Team will:
- Gather information about current family services (if applicable).
- Write a vision statement for family services based on community input.

The Leadership Team should consist of both lay and professional leadership, including a lay chair and a lead professional staff member who understands the broader educational goals of the community.

The chair's tasks include:
- Meeting with synagogue professionals to review and plan approximately three meetings.
- Overseeing Leadership Team meetings.
- Following up with Leadership Team members.

Consider the members of the team carefully. Be sure to invite individuals who offer varied perspectives.

Include parents with children representing the following populations, as applicable:
- Enrolled in religious school
- Enrolled in day school
- Regular attendees of family services
- Infrequent attendees of family services
- Special learning challenges

Also consider whether the team will focus on family services in general or on services for a specific age group (for example, K–2). For general family services, invite parents representing children spanning various age groups. For a specific age group, invite families solely representing that population.

Since most synagogues combine grades for services, note that the following ages typically group well together:
- Preschool (ages 3 and younger)
- Early elementary (ages 4–8)
- Late elementary/middle school (ages 9–12)

Set a positive tone for the team's work together by inviting individuals through either a personal phone call or a warmly written letter. Contact individuals at least four weeks in advance of the first meeting, and send a reminder e-mail one week in advance.

General Guidelines for Running a Good Meeting:
- Confirm attendees.
- Confirm the room, setup, and supply needs.
- Determine supply needs in advance.

- Determine if you wish to have refreshments and if so, who will provide them.
- Create and copy the agenda to distribute at each meeting. Follow the time allocations for each agenda item.
- Begin and end on time.
- Provide name tags or tented name cards for each attendee to use at every meeting.
- Have one participant take minutes to distribute to the group within three days after the meeting. Bring a calendar in order to set a next meeting time.

Phase 1: Self-Reflection and Information Gathering

Meeting #1 ⤳ The Goals of Family Services

Summary: At the first meeting, participants will get to know one another and begin to discuss the goals of communal prayer and family services. They will also learn their roles as members of the Leadership Team. The meeting will conclude with assignments to gather more information about the current or proposed configuration of family services.

Below is a detailed agenda for the meeting chair, including suggested times. Distribute the short bulleted list of agenda items on page 8 to meeting participants or derive your own agenda.

Chair's Agenda

I. B'ruchim Haba'im, Welcome (10 minutes)
- Welcome from the chair.
- Introduction of participants.
- Sharing of team purpose: to create meaningful Shabbat family services.

II. Chavruta, Text Study and Discussion (10 minutes)
Materials: Copies of Text Study sheet: Why Do We Join Together as a Prayer Community?, one per participant (page 9)

Since the team's task concerns the holy work of Shabbat family services, it is appropriate to begin meetings with the study of Jewish text. Traditional Jewish study often takes place in *chavruta*, paired groups. No matter your experience level, *chavruta* provides a safe space for inquiry and discussion.

Guidelines for Chavruta Study:
- Choose a partner.
- Read the text together and discuss the guiding questions.
- Don't be afraid to disagree or to ask follow-up questions of your partner. That's the Jewish tradition of text study!
- The texts are yours, so feel free to write whatever notes you wish on them.

Group Discussion of Text (5 minutes):
Based on these texts, why do we join together in prayer?

III. Identifying Priorities (20 minutes)
Materials: Copies of Identifying Priorities sheet (page 10), one for each participant, pens

Instructions:
- Distribute a copy of the Identifying Priorities sheet to each participant.
- Have participants indicate the five elements of a family service that they value most.
- Discuss and share participants' selections.

IV. Preparing for the Next Meeting: Gathering Information (10 minutes)
Materials: Copies of Informational Survey (pages 11–12), one for each participant. For congregations currently holding family services, also include copies of the State of Our Family Services (pages 13–14).

Through the previous activity, participants identified possible goals for family services and noted their own personal priorities. Now it is time to survey the constituency to identify their goals for family services.

- Distribute copies of the Informational Survey, review, and adjust.
- Assign a committee member the task of sending out the Informational Survey and collecting responses. Responses should be submitted at least two weeks before Meeting #2.
- For congregations that currently hold family services: Complete the State of Our Family Services sheet (pages 13-14), also due at Meeting #2. The data gathered will allow all leadership team members to have the same information about the history and present configuration of family services.
- Invite all team members to attend family services in order to be more informed at Meeting #2.

V. Wrap-Up (5 minutes)
- Distribute a roster of participants' phone numbers and e-mail addresses.
- Confirm the next meeting date.
- Thank participants for their time.

Meeting #1: Agenda

The Goals of Family Services

I. *B'ruchim Haba'im*, Welcome
- Introduction of participants
- Sharing of team purpose: To create meaningful Shabbat family services

II. *Chavruta* Text Study and Discussion: Why Do We Join Together as a Prayer Community?

III. Identifying Priorities
- Identifying Priorities worksheet
- Discussion of selections

IV. Gathering Information
- Informational Survey
- State of Our Family Services

V. Wrap-Up
- Participants' contact information
- Next meeting date and time

Thank you for your participation!

Meeting #1: Text Study

Why Do We Join Together as a Prayer Community?

The following texts discuss various reasons why people join together in prayer communities. As you read and discuss them, consider how their lessons apply to your pursuit of creating a vision for family services.

Guidelines for chavruta (paired) study:
- Choose a partner.
- Read the text together and discuss the guiding questions.
- Don't be afraid to disagree or to ask follow-up questions of your partner. That's the Jewish tradition of text study!
- The texts are yours, so feel free to write whatever notes you wish on them.

Text 1:
"Let my prayer to you, God, be at an acceptable time" (Psalms 69:14). When is "an acceptable time"? The time when the congregation prays.*

Guiding Questions:
- According to this text, what is the connection between communal and individual prayer?
- How might praying together as a congregation also help with individual prayer?

Text 2:
If a calamity falls upon you, you should let your community know so that they can ask for God's mercy on your behalf.**

Guiding Questions:
- What does this text indicate about the role of prayer and community?
- When a community prays on your behalf, what happens?
- In what other ways can a prayer community provide support in times of need? In times of joy?

Text 3:
Parents should teach their children to speak words of Torah and to offer praise to God. ***

Guiding Questions:
- Why is it a parent's responsibility to teach children to study Torah and praise God?
- How do we teach our children to pray?
- What do we want our children to experience during prayer?

---

* Tractate Berachot 8a. Tractate Berachot is a section of the Babylonian Talmud that primarily concerns blessings.

** Tractate Chullin 78a. Tractate Chullin is a section of the Babylonian Talmud that focuses on which animals may be eaten and how they are to be slaughtered.

*** *Sefer Ha'Aggadah*, 635:231. *Sefer Ha'Aggadah* is a collection of the nonlegal contents of the Talmud, including ethical teachings, legends, and folklore.

Meeting #1

Identifying Priorities

Please select what you consider to be the five most important elements of family services.

- They offer an opportunity for parents to spend time with their children.
- They allow families to meet and spend time together.
- They offer opportunities for children to meet other Jewish children.
- They connect families to the congregation.
- They encourage participants to think about and discuss God.
- They teach new, child-friendly tunes for Shabbat.
- They teach traditional songs and melodies.
- They feature a lot of music.
- They prepare children to become *b'nei mitzvah*.
- They offer opportunities for parents to connect or reconnect with Judaism.
- They connect to children's formal religious education.
- They offer creative opportunities for engagement with prayer, Torah, and holidays.
- They focus on the weekly Torah portion or upcoming holiday.
- They offer children opportunities for leadership.

Informational Survey

All congregants:

1. Please fill in: My child/ren's age/s: _____.

For congregations currently holding family services, include questions 2 – 9. If your congregation does not presently hold family services, skip to question 10.

2. Select one: We presently attend family services at our congregation:
   - 0-4 times a year
   - 5-10 times a year
   - 11-20 times a year
   - 21-40 times a year
   - 41-52 times a year

3. Fill in the blank: I get information about family services through: _____
   (for example, the synagogue Web site, newsletter, friends, education director, preschool director)

4. Agree or Disagree: Family services are well-publicized in our synagogue (i.e., people know date and time, people know where services are located upon entering the synagogue)

5. Please answer: How would you describe the current family service you attend?
   _____

6. Please answer: Are people excited about our family services? What have you heard from other people about the service? _____

7. Please answer: Do you know people who are not attending the service who might enjoy or benefit from it? If so, why are they not attending? _____

For all congregations:

8. Select one: It is our preference that services be held: every week, twice a month, once a month, a few times a year, not at all

9. Select one: The ideal length of a service for my family is: 20–30 minutes, 30–45 minutes, 45 minutes–1 hour, 1 1/2 hours.

In each area below (Leadership, Content, etc.), mark the two elements that are most important to you:

Leadership
   a. Parents run the service.
   b. Professional leaders (non-clergy) run the service.
   c. The clergy (i.e., rabbi or cantor) run the service.
   d. The clergy does not lead the service but visits every session.
   e. Teenage assistants are present.
   f. There is an opportunity for me as a parent to receive training to lead the service.

Content
    a. Age-appropriate Jewish stories (not necessarily about the Torah portion) are told.
    b. Someone reads from a Torah scroll during the service.
    c. There is discussion of the weekly Torah story or upcoming holiday.
    d. There is creative or dramatic interpretation of the weekly Torah portion.
    e. An age-appropriate siddur (prayer book) is used in the service.
    f. The service offers transliterations of the words of the prayers.
    g. The prayer tunes are the familiar, traditional tunes used in adult services.
    h. There is a lot of singing in the service.
    i. The service includes non-liturgical Jewish songs written for children.
    j. If permitted on Shabbat in your synagogue, worshippers use percussion instruments (for example, drums and shakers).
    k. If permitted on Shabbat in your synagogue, worshippers use non-percussion instruments (for example, guitar).

Structure
    a. The leaders encourage me to drop off my child at the service.
    b. The leaders encourage me to stay with my child at the service.
    c. Babysitting is available in addition to family services.

Goals
    a. I meet new families at the service.
    b. I see the same families every week at the service.
    c. Everyone in the service knows my name and my child's name.
    d. The service provides me the opportunity to spend time with my child.
    e. My child has the chance to spend time with other Jewish children.
    f. It prepares my child to become a bar or bat mitzvah.
    g. It introduces children to the culture of our congregation.
    h. It allows an opportunity for me and my family to talk about God.
    i. I have an opportunity to connect/reconnect with and learn more about Judaism.

After Family Services
    a. There is a separate *oneg/kiddush* for family service participants.
    b. The family services join the main congregation for *kiddush*.
    c. There is a place for children to play after family services conclude and before adult services end.
    d. Children are invited into the adult services to help conclude the service (for example, lead Adon Olam or Ein Keloheinu).

Fill in: What additional suggestions or recommendations do you have?

_____

_____

_____

State of Our Family Services

Past and Present

I. The History of Our Family Services
- When did they begin? Who founded them? What was their stated goal?

II. Our Family Services Today
- Which family services are available? What are the intended children's age groups? How many children attend?
- Is babysitting also available? If so, when does babysitting take place?

If there is more than one service, answer the following questions for each service.

Publicity
- What is the name of the service?
- How is the service publicized? (Be as specific as possible, bringing in flyers or information from the synagogue Web site.)

Schedule
- How many times per month do family services take place?
- At what time do family services begin and end? What time do adult services begin and end?
- Do family services begin and end on time?

Location
- Where do services take place? (*classroom, sanctuary, chapel*) What does the physical space look like? (*pews, movable chairs, rug, windows*)
- How flexible is the location? Are other spaces available? If so, what are the pros and cons of those spaces?

Attendees
- How many families attend on average?
- Who currently attends the service? What are the ages of the children? Do they come with their parents? Do both parents (if applicable) attend, or just one?
- Is there a synagogue or religious school requirement for students to attend services? If so, what is the policy? Is the policy followed?

Relationship to Adult Service
- What occurs in the adult service while family services are taking place?
- Is there an announcement in the main sanctuary that family services are about to begin?
- Do children play a role in the adult service? (*lead Adon Olam, lead Ein Keloheinu*)

Community
- How are families welcomed to the service? (*ushers, welcome by the leader as they enter, an opening song*)
- How many "regulars" attend each service?
- How many visitors attend each service? How do visitors hear about the services?
- Do families know each others' names? Do they socialize outside of the service? Do they receive each others' contact information?

Leadership
- Who leads the service? (*senior or assistant rabbi, cantor, education director, ritual director, lay leaders, teens*) What training, preparation, and resources do the service leaders receive?
- What is the role of clergy in the service?
- What is the role of teens in the service?

Content
- Does the service have its own *siddur* (prayer book)? Who created it? Does it include transliterations?
- Which prayers, and in what order, does the leader cover each week? Be specific.
- How much of the service consists of prayers? How much of Shabbat-related songs?
- How much of the service is in Hebrew? How much in English?
- How is the physical Torah used in the service? (*a real Torah is used in the service, the service has its own Ark and Torah scroll*)

Style
- How does the leader incorporate instruments/music in the service?
- How does the leader incorporate movement (for example, dancing, stretching) in the service?
- How are stories and storytelling used? Does the leader read stories from a book or tell them aloud? Do stories connect to the Torah portion or upcoming holiday, or do they contain general Jewish content, such as values, rituals, and customs? Are stories generally below, at, or above age level of attendees?
- How are props (for example, puppets, stuffed Torahs) used in the service?
- What is the balance between the voice of the leader and the voice of the congregation in the service? How does it compare to the balance in the general service?

After the Service
- Is there an *oneg* specifically for the family service? If so, who organizes it?
- Who leads the community in Kiddush over grape juice and Hamotzi over challah?
- Who makes announcements about upcoming programs after the service?
- Is there a designated play space for attendees of family services? If so, where is that space and what occurs there?
- When a family graduates from this service, where do they go?

Buzz
- What is the "word on the street" about the service? How might a regular attendee describe it? An occasional attendee?
- Who *isn't* coming to the service who might enjoy or benefit from it? Why aren't they attending?

Phase 2: Writing a Vision Statement for Family Services

Meeting #2 — Writing a Family Services Vision Statement

Summary: This meeting will reveal multiple opinions about the purpose of family services. Participants will discuss the results of the information gathering. The meeting will conclude with participants working together to create a draft vision statement for family services.

Below is a detailed agenda for the meeting chair, including suggested times. Distribute the short bulleted list of agenda items on page 16 to meeting participants or derive your own agenda.

Chair's Agenda

I. B'ruchim Haba'im, Welcome (5 minutes)
- Welcome participants and have them reintroduce themselves

II. *Chavruta*, Text Study and Discussion (5 minutes)
Materials: Copies of Text Study sheet: For the Sake of Community, one per participant (page 17)

III. State of Our Family Services (25 minutes)
Materials: Summary of survey results (provided by volunteers)
- Pre-assigned volunteer presents summary results from the Informational Survey and/or State of Our Family Services. (You will use these results at meeting #3.) Discuss the results.

Guidelines for Discussion:
- This conversation is not about judging or fixing; it is about sharing information so that all participants have the same level of understanding of current family services.
- Comments and questions should be clarifying and fact-based (not problem-solving).
- If a major issue with the current state of family services emerges, note it for later discussion.

IV. Writing a Preliminary Vision Statement (20 minutes)
Materials: Chart paper; markers; copy of Sample Vision Statements, one per participant (page 18)
- Have the group begin to write a preliminary vision statement based on the survey results.
- Remind participants that a vision statement is a brief statement (3–5 sentences) that describes what an organization wants to become. It is future-oriented. The vision statement helps participants make decisions, because, as much as possible, each action taken should align with the vision. In our case, the vision statement will guide each element of the design of family services.
- Write at the top of the chart paper: "Family Services at [congregation name]." Have participants offer phrases that reflect the key points of the survey results. For example, if survey results indicated that respondents prefer clergy-led services with traditional liturgical tunes and creative interpretations of the Torah portion, write: "clergy-led," "featuring traditional liturgical tunes," and "creative interpretations of the Torah portion." Summarize the phrases in a short paragraph.

Guidelines:
- Remember that a vision statement reflects each congregation's unique culture and values.
- A vision statement cannot address every possible detail of family services. Therefore, this exercise requires making decisions about the most common themes of the survey results.
- See Sample Vision Statements (page 18) for examples from other congregations.
- Vision statements are future-oriented, so some elements may not be attainable *right now*. Rather, it describes where the team would like family services to be one day.

V. Wrap-Up (5 minutes)
- Assign a volunteer to take the statement written on the chart paper and edit as needed. Assign a few representatives from the Leadership Team to attend the next two meetings.
- Take time to recognize each member's participation in the process of writing a vision statement.

Meeting #2: Agenda

Writing a Family Services Vision Statement

I. *B'ruchim Haba'im*, Welcome
- Reintroduction of participants

II. *Chavruta* Text Study and Discussion: For the Sake of Community

III. The State of Our Family Services
- Presentation of results from "Informational Survey" and/or "State of Our Family Services"
- Discussion of results

IV. Writing a Preliminary Vision Statement
- Sample vision statements
- As a group, write a 3–5 sentence, future-oriented vision statement based on summary of survey results

V. Wrap-Up

Thank you for your participation!

Meeting #2: Text Study

For the Sake of the Community

When people work together, at times there may be tension between an individual's needs and desires and those of the larger group. The text below refers to the time in Jewish history when priests served in the Temple; part of their job was to offer blessings to the people. One lesson we can take from the text is that when tension or conflict exists, the needs of the community take precedence.

Guidelines for chavruta (paired) study:
- Choose a partner.
- Read the text together and discuss the guiding questions.
- Don't be afraid to disagree or to ask follow-up questions of your partner. That's the Jewish tradition of text study!
- The texts are yours, so feel free to write whatever notes you wish on them.

Rabbi Isaac said: Let respect for the community always be with you, for when the priests blessed worshippers during the Priestly Blessing,* the priests' faces were turned toward the people while their backs were toward the Presence [God]. **

Guiding Questions:
- How do the priests show respect for the community in the above text?
- What does this text teach about leadership, specifically about the relationship between leaders and the community?
- What lessons does this text offer us as members of a leadership team as we write a vision for our congregation's family services?

---

* The Priestly Blessing, also known as the Kohanic Blessing or Birkat Kohanim, comes from Numbers 6:22-27. It is a tripartite blessing that God instructs the *kohanim* to offer to the people Israel: "May God bless you and protect you. May God be kind and gracious to you. May God bestow favor upon you and grant you peace!" In the ancient Temple, the priests recited the blessing twice daily while facing the people. In some traditional communities today, descendants of the *kohanim* still offer the blessing on Shabbat and holidays.

** Tractate Sotah 40a.

Meeting #2

Sample Vision Statements

> ### What Is a Vision Statement?
>
> A vision statement is a brief statement (3-5 sentences) that describes what an organization wants to become. It is future-oriented. The vision statement helps participants make decisions, because, as much as possible, each action taken should align with the vision. In our case, the vision statement will guide each element of the design of family services.

1. Temple Beth Am's family services provide opportunities for parents and children to spend time together as they gain familiarity with traditional tunes and with the welcoming culture of Beth Am.

2. Emanu-El's family services serve to foster parent leadership as parents experiment with new tunes and worship techniques to engage our children in exciting worship experiences that are pedagogically sound.

3. Congregation Shaarey Shalom's family services are professionally led with a focus on the Torah service and Torah/holiday stories. In addition to keeping families sensitive to the cycle of the Jewish year, the focus on the Torah service will help children with preparation for their *b'nei mitzvah*.

Note that each statement describes a very different congregation, its unique culture and values. Also note that the vision statements do not describe all the details of the service. Rather, they set a general tone for what the service will feel like.

Meeting #3: Expanding Our Vision

Summary: This meeting is designed for a small group of key individuals, including the chair, select Leadership Team members, and the education director and/or rabbi. They will review the Informational Survey results and the vision statement developed by the Leadership Team, and begin to expand it by asking the questions: "If our vision is achieved, what will our services look like? Feel like? Sound like?"

Below is a detailed agenda for the meeting chair, including suggested times. Distribute the short bulleted list of agenda items on page 20 to meeting participants or derive your own agenda.

Chair's Agenda

I. B'ruchim Haba'im, Welcome (5 minutes)
- Welcome participants and have them reintroduce themselves.

II. Chavruta, Text Study and Discussion (10 minutes)
Materials: Copies of Text Study sheet: Working Together, one per participant (page 21)

III. Our Vision Statement
Materials: Copies of the vision statement typed up from the last meeting, one per participant
- Distribute the vision statement from the Leadership Team meeting.
- As a group, refine and clarify the vision statement, respecting the Leadership Team's efforts and hard work.

Guidelines for Discussion:
- Ask only questions that clarify. Clarifying questions should relate to specific words or phrasing in the statement.
- Refer to Sample Vision Statements (page 18) if needed.
- Rewrite the statement in a form that acknowledges any changes.

IV. Expanding Our Vision (20 minutes)
Utilizing the Informational Survey results and the revised vision statement, this smaller group will now expand upon the vision statement to create a more nuanced picture of Shabbat family services.

Materials: Team's most complete version of the vision statement on the board or a large sheet of paper; summary of Informational Survey results; copies of Expanding Our Vision Statement Worksheet, one per participant (page 22); pens; Sample Expanded Vision Statements (pages 23–25)

Directions:
- Review results of the Informational Survey conducted by the Leadership Team to best reflect respondents' needs and desires in a family service.
- Distribute copies of Expanding Our Vision Statement Worksheets (page 22) for participants to complete.
- Refer to Sample Expanded Vision Statements (pages 23–25) for guidance.
- As a group, compose an expanded vision statement. Assign a volunteer to write down the expanded vision statement, which will be shared with the service leader at the next meeting.

V. Wrap-Up (10 minutes)
- Take time to recognize each member's contribution to the process.

Meeting #3: Agenda

Expanding Our Vision

I. *B'ruchim Haba'im*, Welcome
- Reintroduction of participants

II. *Chavruta* Text Study and Discussion: Working Together

III. Our Vision Statement
- Review vision statement
- As a group, refine vision statement

IV. Expanding Our Vision
- Expanding Our Vision Statement worksheet
- Sample Expanded Vision Statements

V. Wrap-Up

Thank you for your participation!

Meeting #3: Text Study

Working Together

The rabbis encouraged their students to have heated discussions and argue respectfully, recognizing that the process of working something out with another person is as important as the conclusion at which they arrive.

Guidelines for chavruta (paired) study:
- Choose a partner.
- Read the text together and discuss the guiding questions.
- Don't be afraid to disagree or to ask follow-up questions of your partner. That's the Jewish tradition of text study!
- The texts are yours, so feel free to write whatever notes you wish on them.

Rabbi Chama son of Chanina said: What is meant by the verse: "Iron sharpens iron" [Proverbs 27:17]? It means that one piece of iron sharpens another; so, too, do two scholars sharpen each others' minds when they discuss Jewish law.

Rabah son of Chana said: Why are the words of Torah likened to fire, as in the verse, "Is not my word like fire, says God" [Jeremiah 23:29]? To teach you that just as fire does not ignite of itself, so too, words of Torah do not flourish in the one who studies alone.*

Guiding Questions:
- The first part of the text describes two scholars sharpening each others' minds. How does such sharpening occur when two people study together?
- What does the second part of the text teach us about working alone versus working with others?
- What lessons do these texts offer as we work together to write a vision statement for our family services?

---

* Tractate Ta'anit 7a

Meeting #3

Expanding Our Vision Statement Worksheet

This exercise will help us better picture how the vision statement will be applied by asking: "When we achieve this vision, what will our family services look like? Feel like? Sound like?"

Write our vision statement here:

Now divide the vision statement into phrases, writing each phrase in its own box. Answer the questions about each phrase.

Write a phrase of our vision statement here:
If we achieve this element of our vision, what will our family services look, feel, and sound like?

Write a phrase of our vision statement here:
If we achieve this element of our vision, what will our family services look, feel, and sound like?

Write a phrase of our vision statement here:
If we achieve this element of our vision, what will our family services look, feel, and sound like?

Meeting #3

Expanded Vision Statement
Sample 1
Temple Beth Am

Write our vision statement here:
Temple Beth Am's family services provide opportunities for parents and children to spend time together as they gain familiarity with traditional tunes and with the welcoming culture of Beth Am.

Now divide the vision statement into phrases, writing each phrase in its own box. Answer the questions about each phrase.

Write a phrase of our vision statement here:
"Provide opportunities for parents and children to spend time together"

If we achieve this element of our vision, what will our family services look, feel, and sound like?

- Families will sit on the floor as a small group.
- The service will allow time for parents and children to reflect on the week together.
- The leader will address the parents in the service and will not merely "entertain" the children.
- Parents and children will feel comfortable singing along and leading together.

Write a phrase of our vision statement here:
"as they gain familiarity with traditional tunes"

If we achieve this element of our vision, what will our family services look, feel, and sound like?

- The leader, an active layperson or a clergy member, will know the tunes and traditional order of prayers at Beth Am.
- The leader will post MP3s of the prayers and songs on the Beth Am Web site so that families can download and listen to them.
- The prayers will follow the same order each week.
- Transliterations and musical notations for the prayers will be available.

Write a phrase of our vision statement here:
"and with the welcoming culture of Beth Am"

If we achieve this element of our vision, what will our family services look, feel, and sound like?

- A designated volunteer usher from the community will welcome families each week.
- Regular attendees will have nametags, and visitors will be asked their names and receive nametags at the next service.
- At the beginning and end of each service, participants will share their names.
- New families will receive a welcome at the *oneg* or *kiddush* from an assigned "buddy family."

Meeting #3

Expanded Vision Statement
Sample 2
Congregation Emanu-El

Write our vision statement here:
Emanu-El's family services serve to foster parent leadership as parents experiment with new tunes and worship techniques to engage our children in exciting worship experiences that are pedagogically sound.

Write a phrase of our vision statement here:
"serve to foster parent leadership"

If we achieve this element of our vision, what will our family services look, feel, and sound like?
- Parents will lead the service (ideally in pairs: a new leader and a more experienced leader).
- Parents will sign up online for leading to democratize the process.
- Experienced parents will be available for consultation before services so that new leaders can feel confident and prepared.

Write a phrase of our vision statement here:
"as parents experiment with new tunes and techniques"

If we achieve this element of our vision, what will our family services look, feel, and sound like?
- The service will feel different each week, with some core anchor prayers.
- Parents will add their strengths to the service. An actor parent might help the children act out the Torah portion; an artist could create a tent of cloth under which the children sit for Mah Tovu.
- Parents will introduce new tunes or write their own tunes for prayers.

Write a phrase of our vision statement here:
"to engage our children in exciting worship experiences"

If we achieve this element of our vision, what will our family services look, feel, and sound like?
- Services will feel energetic.
- Children's opinions will be taken into account so that they feel part of the service as well.

Write a phrase of our vision statement here:
"that are pedagogically sound"

If we achieve this element of our vision, what will our family services look, feel, and sound like?
- Parents will consider the ages of the children attending the service and adjust accordingly.
- Expert educators will be consulted to offer activity and discussion ideas.

Meeting #3

Expanded Vision Statement
Sample 3
Temple Shaarey Shalom

Write our vision statement here:
Congregation Shaarey Shalom's family services are professionally led with a focus on the Torah service and Torah/holiday stories. In addition to keeping families sensitive to the cycle of the Jewish year, the focus on the Torah service will help children with preparation for their *b'nei mitzvah*.

Write a phrase of our vision statement here:
"professionally led"

If we achieve this element of our vision, what will our family services look, feel, and sound like?

- A professional, experienced Jewish educator leads services.
- The rabbi and cantor will supervise the service and the professional leader.

Write a phrase of our vision statement here:
"with a focus on the Torah service and Torah/holiday stories"

If we achieve this element of our vision, what will our family services look, feel, and sound like?

- The Torah service will be the centerpiece of the service (approximately 75% of the service will be dedicated to the Torah service in some fashion).
- The name of the Torah portion and the book of the Torah in which it is found (for example, Parashat No'ach in the book of Genesis) will be mentioned prominently each week.
- The leader will read a few verses from the Torah portion each week.
- The leader will provide a sheet of Torah-related questions for families to take home and discuss.

Write a phrase of our vision statement here:
"keeping families sensitive to the cycle of the Jewish year"

If we achieve this element of our vision, what will our family services look, feel, and sound like?

- Songs and stories will teach families about upcoming holidays.
- The leader will note special Torah readings (for example, for holidays).
- When we complete a book of the Torah (for example, the end of Genesis), the community will recite the traditional statement, *Chazak Chazak V'Nitchazek*.
- We will sing a Jewish calendar song that lists the order of the Jewish months at every new Jewish month.

Write a phrase of our vision statement here:
"will help children with preparation for their *b'nei mitzvah*"

If we achieve this element of our vision, what will our family services look, feel, and sound like?

- Children will have an opportunity to lead the Torah service after meeting with the service leader.
- Children will have the opportunity to read verses from the Torah after consultation with the service leader.
- In anticipation of their assigned bar/bat mitzvah portion, children will be asked to give a *d'var Torah* on the portion.

Phase 3: Implementing Our Family Service

Summary: In this phase, the chair, a small group of representatives from the Leadership Team, and the education director and/or rabbi will present the expanded vision statement to the service leader. Together, this group of key individuals will consider and design each element of the service. At regular intervals after implementation, they will request feedback from the full Leadership Team and adjust the service accordingly.

If there is more than one leader leading services for different ages, hold separate meetings with each.

In this meeting:
- Review and discuss the expanded vision statement.
- Refer to a siddur and/or an outline of the Shabbat morning service (see Appendix for suggested outlines) to determine the prayers that you will use in the service. Consider the length and goals of the service.
- For each prayer, consider the suggestions offered in Part Two of this guide (beginning on page 27) to determine appropriate activities for your service.
- Remember to continually check the vision statement to make sure that activities correspond with the vision statement and the age group that will be served.
- Make sure that the service leader knows the tunes the congregation sings.
- Plan the service.
- If desired, choose a name that reflects the new spirit of this service.

Prior to the formal launch of the service:
- Rehearse the service with the service leader, preferably in the room where the service will take place.
- Advertise the service in the community (bulletin, e-mail, announcement in local newspaper).

On the day of the service:
- Celebrate the inauguration of the service with a special *oneg* or *kiddush*.
- Be sure to recognize all individuals who have contributed to the creation of the service.

At regular intervals after the launch of the service:
- Have members of the Leadership Team attend family services to ensure that the service aligns with the vision statement.
- Invite feedback, including concerns and comments about the service, through open community meetings, regular surveys, the synagogue Web site, and periodic direct observations of the service by Leadership Team members.
- Make adjustments to the service as needed.

Part Two

For the Service Leader
Enriching Your Services

Family services offer a unique opportunity for creative expression and experiential learning. In this section, you will find many suggestions for integrating prayer with personal reflection, art, movement, and music in order to make prayer more accessible—and fun—for adults and children alike.

Take a moment to consider the vision and goals of your family service. Keep these goals in mind as you review this section. Remember that not all ideas are right for your community, or for your community right now. Be willing to experiment, and also be patient with the pace of change.

In this section, you will find:
- General tips for service leaders on planning, preparing, and opening services
- Summaries and activity suggestions for prayers frequently used in family services

Note on art: All suggestions offered under the "incorporating art" section refer to paintings in *Siddur Mah Tov* (Behrman House, 2010), a family Shabbat prayer book featuring full-page, full-color, original acrylic paintings that illustrate the themes of the prayers.

Note on music: Services can be enriched by new tunes and songs. For ideas, speak with your cantor or check the Web for additional resources.

Note on activities: Some of the following activities were contributed by experienced educators, rabbis, ritual directors, and service leaders. Each contribution is indicated by a numbered footnote. All contributors are credited on page 46.

General Planning Tips for Service Leaders

Prepare!

- Check the calendar: consider the upcoming Torah portion, and note if there are any upcoming holidays (Jewish or secular), or national or local events of interest to the community.
- When planning the year, schedule special programming, such as Grandparents' Shabbat or Special Friend Shabbat.
- Make a list of the prayers you will include and how long you expect each to take. For services for children ages 3 years and younger, 35-40 minutes is optimal. For services for children ages 4 and older, 45-60 minutes is a good length.
- Practice reading/telling any stories aloud.
- Review the melodies that you will use in the service. Ask the cantor if you can practice with him or her or listen to recordings of the tunes.
- Develop short transitions between the end of one prayer and the beginning of another; congregants do not want lengthy introductions to or explanations of prayers.
- Consider how to adjust the service if the children attending are younger or older than expected.
- Create backup plans (extra stories, songs, or games) in case you have extra time at the end.
- Check the weather: a very warm or very cold day can affect attendance as well as the mood of participants. Plan the physical environment accordingly.

Be flexible!

- Be aware that since participants do not RSVP for family services, the number and types of attendees may constantly change.
- Remember that children are unpredictable. What works one week might not work the next.
- Wait a few seconds after asking a question; if you get no response, rephrase your question or move on.
- A good sense of humor is invaluable. If you forget the words to a song or start singing in a key that is too high for your register, laugh at yourself—it helps you and others feel comfortable. Remember that this is a community experience, not a performance.
- After the service, take time to reflect alone and with participants on what worked and didn't work, and make notes for next time.

Room Setup

Family services can take place in any space. No matter where you are, prepare the room as a holy space. Consider whether and how to use the following:

- Chairs (and whether to provide adult and/or children's seating)
- A rug or pillows on the floor
- An Ark and/or a real or toy Torah
- Prayer books (Toddlers can follow along with a large illustrated prayer book at the front of the room; from kindergarten-age on, children can proudly hold their own prayer book. In all cases, provide adults the opportunity to follow along with their own prayer book.)
- Other props, such as musical instruments (if permitted on Shabbat in your synagogue), shakers, flags, a play Shabbat set, and puppets

🕊 Welcoming Families

Before you begin, the service leader and regular attendees can help welcome newcomers and create community in the following ways:

- Ensure that signs posted for the family service location are clear and accurate.
- Designate parent ushers to welcome attendees.
- Greet everyone with a big smile and a short, personal greeting.
- Be ready to welcome the early birds. Start on time out of respect for those who arrive punctually. Consider opening with a few warm-up songs like "Bim Bam" or "Mah Yafeh Hayom" and doing a formal welcome for the whole group ten minutes into the service. As latecomers arrive, greet them with a smile and a wave while continuing the flow of the service.
- Warmly welcome all participants, noting that this is an environment where people of all backgrounds, religions, and knowledge levels are welcome and encouraged to participate.
- Have everyone briefly introduce themselves early on in the service to someone they do not know.
- Begin the service with a short story or the beginning of a story that can be continued at a later point in the service. [i]

🕊 Building the Prayer Service

In this section, you will find a breakdown of the prayers traditionally used in family services, including:

- A brief summary of each prayer's content or context
- Specific ideas for enriching your service by incorporating art, movement, narrative, and props
- Suggested guiding questions for discussion

The prayers are those included in *Siddur Mah Tov: A Family Shabbat Prayer Book* (Behrman House, 2010). Page numbers apply to both the Conservative (C) and Reform (R) editions. When the page numbers differ, the edition is specified. You can, of course, use the ideas with *any* prayer book or even with no prayer book at all.

Modeh/Modah Ani
🕊 Page 4

Modeh/Modah Ani is a prayer thanking God for returning our souls to us in the morning. Gratitude is an essential part of Jewish prayer. *Note:* Boys and men say *modeh ani*; girls and women say *modah ani*.

Incorporating Art
Direct participants to look in *Siddur Mah Tov* at the illustration of the child waking up and ask:

- What were you thankful for when you woke up this morning?
- What are you looking forward to today?

Incorporating Movement

- Guide families in simple physical stretches while singing Modeh/Modah Ani together. Stretching wakes us as we connect our actions to the words of the prayer. You can also incorporate Hebrew, for example, "circle your *rosh* [head]," "stretch your *yadayim* [hands]."

Mah Tovu
🕊 Page 6

Mah Tovu comes from the Torah (Numbers 24:5). These words were recited by a non-Jewish prophet named Balaam. He was hired to curse the Jews but found himself able only to utter words of blessing. We traditionally recite Mah Tovu upon entering the synagogue.

Incorporating Art

The painting accompanying Mah Tovu in *Siddur Mah Tov* is a scene of tents in the desert, depicting where the ancient Israelites lived. Ask participants:

- What do we use tents for? *(camping, shelter)*
- How are synagogues like tents? *(they are places where we can be together with our families, where we can be safe)*
- How are tents unlike synagogues? *(tents are temporary, they offer limited shelter from the elements, they are not sturdy)*
- The Israelites gathered together in tents to tell stories and feel safe in community. What makes you feel safe?
- Abraham and Sarah practiced the value of *hachnasat orchim*; they welcomed guests into their tent. How do you welcome others into your homes and communities? *(introduce ourselves, invite others to play with us, offer food and drink, ask others about themselves)*

Incorporating Movement

- While singing, have congregants put their arms over their heads as if making a tent.

Incorporating Discussion/Narrative

- Read a children's version of the story of Balak, Balaam, and the talking donkey (Numbers 22:2-24:25), which is the source of Mah Tovu.

Incorporating Props

- Gather the children underneath a large tallit (prayer shawl) while singing Mah Tovu. The imagery of children underneath a tallit, as they may one day be under a *chupah* (wedding canopy), is emotional for many parents. You may use a colorful parachute instead of a tallit, providing an opportunity to review Hebrew colors.

Hinei Mah-Tov

📖 Page 6

Hinei Mah-Tov, an excerpt from Psalm 133, celebrates community coming together with a message that resonates with people of all faiths ("how wonderful it is when friends and family come together").

Incorporating Movement

- Have family members put their arms around one another and sway while singing Hinei Mah-Tov.

Incorporating Discussion/Narrative

- Ask participants: How many of you have brothers and sisters? Is your brother or sister in the room? How do you feel knowing that we are all brothers and sisters in that we all share the same ancient ancestors *(we are all part of the human family)*?

Incorporating Props

- Bring in pictures of people from different backgrounds and cultures and ask participants: How are these people all brothers and sisters? *(they are all part of the human family; we are all made in the image of God, b'tzelem Elohim)* What are their responsibilities to one another? *(to treat each other with respect; to take care of the earth, our communal home; to help those who are less fortunate than we)*

Birchot Hashachar

 Page 8

Birchot Hashachar is a series of morning blessings that prepare us for the day. The rabbis of the Talmud offered a variety of blessings that reflect the process of waking. They range from thanking God for giving the rooster the ability to distinguish between day and night (and in turn waking people) to thanking God for giving us the strength to rise from our beds. Each blessing in Birchot Hashachar begins with the six-word Hebrew formula, *Baruch Atah Adonai Eloheinu Melech ha'olam…* (Praised are You, God, Ruler of the universe…), followed by a reason that we are thankful. *Siddur Mah Tov* includes many, but not all, of the blessings in Birchot Hashachar. Choose those that will resonate with your congregation. Tradition teaches that we should recite 100 blessings a day, and reciting Birchot Hashachar is a great way to start!

Incorporating Art

- In *Siddur Mah Tov*, point to the illustration of the rooster and ask the children: Did a rooster wake you this morning? Did you wake up some other way? How?

Incorporating Movement

- Since Birchot Hashachar reflects the process of waking, you can easily incorporate physical movement. For *pokei'ach ivrim* (who opens our eyes), participants can close and open their eyes. For *malbish arumim* (who clothes us), they can point to their clothes. Either the leader or the children can create appropriate corresponding motions.

Incorporating Discussion/Narrative

- Have participants offer their own morning blessings.
- Ask individuals to offer a "Shehecheyanu moment"—something new or exciting they experienced during the week.
- Have participants share something for which they are thankful, and then offer together the umbrella blessing, *Baruch Atah Adonai Eloheinu Melech ha'olam, she'asah li kol tzorki* (Praised are You, God, Ruler of the universe, who provides for my every need).

Incorporating Props

- The rooster in *Siddur Mah Tov* is one possible visual image for this series of blessings. However, Birchot Hashachar is replete with imagery. Using a computer, magazine pictures, or your own drawings, create illustrations of the different Birchot Hashachar blessings.
- *B'rachah* Beads (*materials:* 1 bag holding 100 beads of various colors, string for beading). The rabbis teach that we should say 100 blessings a day. Invite participants to count the blessings (both communal and individual) recited, beginning with Birchot Hashachar and continuing until the end of the service. After each blessing, invite a child to string a bead (or to add beans to a pot). At the end of the service, participants will count the beads (or beans) and then determine how many more blessings they still have to say to reach 100. The group can then brainstorm other moments during the day when they might say a blessing.[ii]

Psalm 150

 Page 10

Psalm 150 is one in a series of psalms recited as part of P'sukei D'zimra—verses of praise. The psalm encourages us to praise God through music and dance. Congregations that use instruments on Shabbat can introduce live instruments with this psalm; others can discuss how we use music, our bodies, and other modalities to pray.

Incorporating Art
- Have children look at the painting and describe what they see. (*a boy, a girl, instruments, a shofar, a violin, swirls indicating sound and movement*)
- Usually we use words to pray. The children in the painting are showing us a different way to pray. Ask participants: What are other ways we can pray or speak to God? (*music, song, dance, art, clapping, humming, poetry, silently, with movement*)

Incorporating Movement
- Have students pantomime the instruments mentioned in Psalm 150. To assist with this, create posters with pictures of the various instruments. Write the names of the instruments in Hebrew and English on the front of the posters for the participants and on the back for your reference. As you sing Psalm 150, hold up the pictures and have participants pantomime using them.
- Psalm 150 refers to dance as a way to praise God. Use a catchy melody to get participants up and dancing.

Incorporating Discussion/Narrative
- Ask the group: We talk to God through prayer, and also through music, dance, and art. How many of you are musicians, dancers, or artists? How do these activities help you feel closer to God?
- Ask the group: Psalm 150 is part of a group of morning blessings that help us warm up to pray. What do you warm up for? (*baseball, ballet, piano, soccer*) Why is it important to prepare before doing something important? (*gets us ready, focuses us, limbers us up, allows us to do our best*)
- Psalm 150 ends with the phrase *kol han'shamah t'haleil Yah*—let every soul praise God. Ask the group: Do you think that animals praise God, and if so, how? (*animals praise God in their language, i.e., by roaring, barking, meowing, the way we praise God in ours; when animals take care of their young, they honor and praise God*)

Incorporating Props
- Many psalms use beautiful metaphors to describe God. To introduce participants to metaphorical language for God, have participants create their own metaphors. Place items around the room (*rock, umbrella, blanket, walking staff, bread*). Ask participants to stand next to the item that best represents how they view God's role in their lives and to explain why they chose that item. (*a rock of strength, an umbrella against hard times, a security blanket, a support system, a provider*)[iii]
- Psalm Poetry (*materials:* sets of index cards written with words commonly found in the psalms [*God, Halleluyah, praise, great, mighty, heaven, earth, thanks, holy, powerful*], words describing things for which children are often thankful [*family, nature, health, toys*], as well as commonly used articles [*the, it, and, for, with*]). The psalms tend to use poetic language to praise God. Have participants practice "writing" their own psalms. Divide children into groups and give them each a set of Psalm Poetry cards. Give each group 10 minutes to put words together into their own "psalm" praising God.[iv]

V'nomar Lefanav and Hal'lu-Hodu LaShem

⮞ Page 12 (C)

"Halleluyah" is another way of saying "thank you" to God. Together V'nomar Lefanav and Hal'lu-Hodu LaShem urge us to sing a new song before God. (Note: these two prayers appear only in the Conservative version of *Siddur Mah Tov*.)

Incorporating Art
- Tell participants that "Halleluyah" is another way of saying "thank you" to God. Hold up the picture and ask: How are the children in the image saying "thank you"? What can you tell about the mood of this prayer from the picture? (*it is upbeat and celebratory; the children are happy, moving and dancing*)

Incorporating Movement
- Encourage participants to put the words of V'nomar Lefanav to a more commonly known tune (such as "Twinkle, Twinkle Little Star"). How does it feel to sing a "new song" before God?
- When singing Hal'lu-Hodu LaShem, have families crouch down when singing *hal'luyah* and jump up on *hodu laShem*.

Bar'chu
Page 12 (R), Page 14 (C)

After warming up, the Bar'chu marks the formal beginning of the prayer service. It is a chance for the leader to invite the group to pray. By responding *Baruch Adonai ham'vorach l'olam va'ed!* the group agrees that it is now time to pray. The Bar'chu traditionally requires a minyan (a group of ten adults). We face east, toward the Ark, when reciting the Bar'chu.

Incorporating Movement
- The choreography of the Bar'chu is as follows: At the word *bar'chu* the leader bends at the knees, at *et* the leader bows from the waist with the upper body and head, and at *Adonai* the leader rises back up. The congregation, reciting the second line, bends their knees and bows at *baruch* and rises up at *Adonai*. The leader uses this same choreography when repeating the congregation's line.
- Invite children to act as leaders, calling the congregation to prayer. An adult can guide the child leaders in the choreography and words of the Bar'chu, while another adult can guide the congregation.

Incorporating Discussion/Narrative
- In the Bar'chu, we call God "the One who is blessed." Ask participants: In what ways do you feel blessed?

Incorporating Props
- Create a posterboard-sized illustration of the choreography of the Bar'chu that participants can refer to during services.

Yotzeir Or
Page 14 (R), Page 16 (C)

In Yotzeir Or, the first blessing before the Sh'ma, we praise God, who "makes light and creates darkness" every day, reminding us of the daily miracle of Creation.

Incorporating Art
- Ask the children what they see in the picture. (*swirling orbs of light, moon, stars, sun*) Teach them the Hebrew words for light (*or*), darkness (*choshech*), sun (*shemesh*), moon (*yarei'ach*), and stars (*kochavim*).

Incorporating Movement
- Teach the group simple signs to help illustrate the prayer. Have participants flip a switch to turn on the lights or pretend they are the sun when they say *or* (light), cover their eyes while saying *choshech* (darkness), make a peace sign with their fingers at *oseh shalom* (makes peace), and open their arms wide at *u'vorei et hakol* (creates everything).

Incorporating Discussion/Narrative
- Many people say they feel close to God when they are in nature or when they see something beautiful like a sunrise or sunset. Ask participants: Why do you think nature makes people feel close to God? (*it reminds them of Creation, it reminds them how small our powers are compared to God's*) When do you feel close to God? (*upon seeing a rainbow, upon seeing a new baby*)
- In the story of Creation in the Bible, God creates light and darkness on the first day, and the moon and sun on the fourth. Read a children's version of the story of Creation and highlight those aspects.
- In the last phrase of Yotzeir Or, we praise God who creates everything—*u'vorei et hakol*. Ask participants: What other aspects of nature are you thankful for? (*new growth in spring, sunny skies, animals*) Indicate that we can include all of these items under the blessing *u'vorei et hakol*.

Ahavah Rabah
🍃 Pages 16, 18 (R), Pages 18, 20 (C)

Ahavah Rabah, the second of two blessings that precede the Sh'ma, tells of God's love for us. It also speaks of ways God guides us, especially through the stories and laws of the Torah.

Incorporating Art
- Point to the large heart in *Siddur Mah Tov*. Ask: What might this prayer be about? (*love*)
- Ask families: The words of Ahavah Rabah suggest that to show us love, God gave us the laws of the Torah to help guide our lives. Which stories and laws in the Torah can help guide you? (*laws of tzedakah, laws about honoring our parents, stories about Adam and Eve taking care of the earth*)

Incorporating Movement
- For communities that use *tallitot*: it is traditional to gather the four corners of the tallit at the end of Ahavah Rabah (at the word *vahavi'einu* in the Conservative version of *Siddur Mah Tov*). Ask four children to help you spread open a tallit and bring the four corners together.

Incorporating Discussion/Narrative
- In Ahavah Rabah, we pray that God helps us become better listeners. How can being a better listener help you be a better person?
- We pray that God helps us both to learn and to teach. What is something you have learned recently? What is something important you have taught someone else?

Sh'ma
🍃 Page 20 (R), Page 22 (C)

The Sh'ma is found in the Torah in the book of Deuteronomy (6:4). Some communities say the Sh'ma with their eyes open, some say it with their eyes closed, and some cover their eyes with their hand while reciting the prayer. Some congregations stand for the Sh'ma, while others remain seated. Some say both lines of the Sh'ma aloud, while others speak or sing the first sentence aloud and recite the second softly.

Incorporating Art
- Younger children, in particular, enjoy pointing out the number 1 in the *Siddur Mah Tov* illustration and connecting it to the words *Adonai Echad* – "God is One."
- The Sh'ma in *Siddur Mah Tov* is written in Torah script because it comes from the Torah. (*Note*: The Torah does not include vowels, but *Siddur Mah Tov* does so to facilitate reading.)

Incorporating Movement
- Teach the group sign language or hand motions that correspond to the words of the Sh'ma.
- Lead a prayer experiment of reciting the Sh'ma in different positions (for example, standing up straight, laying on the floor on your back looking at the ceiling). In each position, chant the Sh'ma together, once with eyes open, then with eyes closed. Discuss with participants which position felt most "prayerful" and why. Remind participants that we can pray in many different positions and at many different times and places. [v]

Incorporating Discussion/Narrative
- When we recite the Sh'ma, we focus on listening. Ask participants: To whom do you listen? (*parents, teachers, community, God*)
- When one sense is impaired, the other senses are heightened. In communities that cover or close their eyes while reciting the Sh'ma, ask: Does covering or closing your eyes help you focus? If so, how? (*when we close our eyes, we are less distracted*)
- The first line of the Sh'ma comes from the Torah. According to the Midrash (rabbinic explanation, Devarim Rabbah 2:35), when Jacob, our biblical ancestor also known as Israel, was on his deathbed, his children recited the Sh'ma. Jacob responded *Baruch sheim k'vod malchuto l'olam va'ed* – "Praised is God, for God is with us always and forever." Ask older children to consider: What response might *you* have to *Sh'ma Yisrael*, "Hear O Israel, Adonai is our God, Adonai is One"?
- Both in the Torah and in *Siddur Mah Tov*, the last letter of the word *Sh'ma* (*ayin*) and the last letter of *Echad* (*dalet*) are enlarged. Together *ayin* and *dalet* spell *eid*, or witness. What are we "witnessing" when we recite the Sh'ma? (*that God is our God, that God is one*)

V'ahavta
⇨ Page 22 (R), Page 24 (C)

The V'ahavta teaches us to love God with all of our heart, soul, and strength. The passage comes from the Torah (Deuteronomy 6:5–9) and is often chanted using trope (traditional Torah chanting musical inflections). Inside the mezuzah on the doorpost of Jewish homes is a parchment that includes the words of the Sh'ma and V'ahavta.

Incorporating Art
- The painting in *Siddur Mah Tov* presents the core elements of the V'ahavta: heart, soul, and strength. Ask participants to look at the painting and indentify those three pieces. If you were the artist, how would you have depicted heart, soul, and strength?

Incorporating Movement
- The V'ahavta features many descriptive words that are easy to pantomime. Teach the group sign language or hand motions that correspond to the words of the V'ahavta. Use the same hand signals each week, and families will quickly learn the words and meaning of the prayer.
- Read the words of the V'ahavta in English and ask participants to act them out as they hear them (for example, for "when you walk on your way," participants may walk around the room; for "when you go to sleep," they may lay on the floor and pretend to sleep).
- If your prayer space has a mezuzah, have students go to the door and find it when reciting "on the doorposts of your house." Students may also count and compare the *mezuzot* in the building as a special activity.

Incorporating Discussion/Narrative
- The V'ahavta commands us to teach our children. Ask children: What do your parents teach you? What can you teach your parents? Ask parents: What values do you want to teach your children? What have your children taught you recently?
- The V'ahavta instructs us to put *mezuzot* on the doorposts of our homes to remind us each time we enter and leave our home that we need to follow God's commandments, including being responsible and kind. Do you think we need such a reminder? Why or why not?
- The V'ahavta says we should love God. How do you show love for God? (*read and honor the Torah, honor parents and siblings, take care of the environment*)
- Identify key verbs in the Hebrew and/or English (*teach, love, walk, speak, sit*), and consider how these verbs relate to the body and to the senses. Have students match each verb to one of the five senses (sight, smell, taste, hearing, touch). Discuss examples of how students use their senses and bodies when doing *mitzvot* or good deeds. (*drinking Shabbat wine/grape juice, listening to others, giving a hug to a friend who is sad*)[vi]

Incorporating Props
- To supplement *Siddur Mah Tov's* illustration of V'ahavta, using computer or hand-drawn images, illustrate the different elements of the prayer. Laminate the pages for long-lasting use.
- Bring in a mezuzah with the back removed to show participants the *klaf*, the parchment paper upon which the verses of the Sh'ma and V'ahavta are written.
- The Sh'ma and V'ahavta are found in *mezuzot* and are also found inside tefillin. Tefillin are black boxes with leather straps that are traditionally wrapped around the head and arm during weekday morning services, to represent the words of the V'ahavta. Bring in a picture or actual set of tefillin to show participants.

Mi Chamochah
Page 26

Mi Chamochah comes from the Torah, from the book of Exodus (15:11). The Torah teaches that after crossing the Sea of Reeds after being freed from slavery in Egypt, the Israelites joyously recited Mi Chamochah. Miriam also led the women in singing with timbrels and dance (Exodus 15:20).

Incorporating Art
- The illustration of Mi Chamochah depicts Miriam and other women dancing at the Sea of Reeds. To show their joy, they danced with timbrels (like a tambourine). Ask: How would you have shown joy at this event? (*dancing, singing, jumping, shouting with joy*)

Incorporating Movement
- Reenact the parting of the sea while singing Mi Chamochah. Set up rows of chairs with a center aisle so that children can lead each other through the sea while singing an upbeat Mi Chamochah.[vii]

Incorporating Discussion/Narrative
- Ask families: What holiday does this remind you of? (*Passover, Pesach*)
- The women brought timbrels and musical instruments with them. Ask: Why do you think they brought instruments with them? (*they anticipated that they would have reason to celebrate; music was such an important part of their lives; they considered instruments essential items to bring*)
- A midrash (rabbinic explanation) teaches that as the Israelites stood at the menacing sea, they were too fearful to move. Finally, a man named Nachshon ben Aminadav approached the water and began to sing *Mi chamochah* as he made his way into it. Some Jews teach that as he entered up to his nose, he coughed out *Mi kamochah, nedar bakodesh* (notice the hard *K* in the second line of the prayer). As he recited *Nora t'hilot*, the waters parted and the Israelites crossed

to freedom. Had it not been for Nachshon's bravery and great faith, perhaps the sea would not have split. Ask the group: What elements of leadership did Nachshon demonstrate? (*initiative, courage, faith; was willing to take a risk*) Even today, we call someone who is willing to take brave risks a "Nachshon."

Incorporating Props
- In communities that use instruments on Shabbat, use shakers or tambourines to reenact the dancing of Miriam and the women while singing Mi Chamochah.
- Invite the children to stand in two lines facing each other, with a volunteer "Nachshon" standing between the heads of both lines. The other children wave their arms like waves. Nachshon begins to cross while saying, *Mi chamochah ba'eilim Adonai*. Nachshon's words cause the waves to settle and be still, allowing Nachshon to cross safely. Each student takes a turn being Nachshon. Students may also use ribbons, blue crepe paper, or plastic sheets to simulate rippling water. [viii]

Amidah
Page 28

Amidah means standing. This prayer is also known as Hat'filah (simply, The Prayer), signifying its central importance in Jewish liturgy. In the first section of the Amidah, we link our lives to those of our ancestors, Abraham, Isaac, Jacob, Sarah, Rebecca, Rachel, and Leah, each of whom had a special relationship with God. Some congregations name the patriarchs only, and not the matriarchs. In the second section, we praise God's power. Next, in the K'dushah, we imitate a choir of angels as we stand with our feet close together and recite, *Kadosh, kadosh, kadosh*—"Holy, holy, holy," as we rise up on our toes three times. Though the Amidah does have a fixed liturgy, it is also a time to offer personal prayers from the heart.

Incorporating Art
- Show the image in *Siddur Mah Tov* of the congregation praying together. Ask participants: What do you see in this picture? Do you think all the people in the picture are experiencing prayer in the same way? How do different people in your congregation pray? How do you pray?

Incorporating Movement
- Teach the choreography of the Amidah. Traditionally, worshippers take three steps backward while saying *Adonai, s'fatai tiftach* and three steps forward when saying *ufi yagid t'hilatecha*. We bow when we say *Baruch Atah Adonai* at the beginning of the first blessing and again at the end (bottom of page 28).

Incorporating Discussion/Narrative
- The Amidah allows time for us to be amazed, feel thankful, and concentrate on things we may need. Ask everyone to think of one thing they experienced this past week that was noteworthy. Have volunteers state their "Wow" out loud in a few words. After each comment, the whole congregation says, "Wow!" Do this again, focusing on something for which each person is grateful. Everyone responds with, "Thanks!" For the third round, each person describes something they hope for or desire. Participants say, "Please!" after each person speaks.[ix] You may choose to point out to adult participants that Shabbat is a time when traditionally we do not ask for things; consequently, the Shabbat Amidah does not include the petitionary prayers of the weekday service.
- Say to the group: With *Adonai s'fatai tiftach*, we pray that God opens our mouths so that we may offer meaningful prayers. This is an opportunity for you to speak with God directly. What prayers in your heart do you wish to offer God today? Share them with others if you wish or say them silently.

Incorporating Props
- Shabbat Stones (*materials:* 1 bowl of small stones, 1 large bowl of water). Place a bowl of small, smooth stones near the door to the room with a sign reading, "Please take one." Before the Amidah, encourage participants to think of their stones as significant memories of their week, either positive experiences or things they would like to put aside for Shabbat. After the Amidah, participants come to the front and place their stones in a bowl of water, allowing the ripples to "pass through" the congregation. Participants may also share their thoughts aloud. The leader says: "By sharing our lives on Shabbat we become a community—a group of people who are a part of each others' lives, who care about each other's joys and sorrows." [x]
- Create puppets, pictures, or paper dolls for the *Avot* and *Imahot* (patriarchs and matriarchs—Abraham, Isaac, Jacob, Sarah, Rebecca, Rachel, and Leah). Use these figures to tell or read stories about our ancestors.
- Create a posterboard-sized illustration of the choreography of the Amidah so that participants can refer to it during services.

Oseh Shalom
◆ Page 32

In Oseh Shalom, we ask God to make peace on earth as it is in heaven. Oseh Shalom traditionally ends the Amidah.

Incorporating Art
- For Oseh Shalom, *Siddur Mah Tov* depicts a dove with an olive branch, a symbol of peace. It refers to the biblical story of Noah and the flood, when the dove, finding dry land, came back with an olive branch in its beak. The dove then came to represent a world renewed.

Incorporating Movement
- Have participants make the letter *shin* with their fingers on one hand (to represent the Hebrew word for peace: *shalom*) and a peace sign with the other to remember the meaning of this song.

Incorporating Discussion/Narrative
- We pray that God helps us make peace. What do you do to help make peace in your family and in the world?

Torah Service
◆ Page 34

The Torah service, a highlight of the Shabbat morning service, can be brief or long, depending on the audience. For younger children, taking out plush Torahs, singing "Torah, Torah, Torah," and reading a Torah- or holiday-related story is exciting. Older children are awed by seeing an actual Torah scroll unrolled and reading from it.

Prepare by knowing the name of the week's *parashah* (portion), the book in which it is located (Genesis, Exodus, etc.), its major characters and narrative, and its themes. For helpful information about the Torah portion and the weekly Haftarah refer to *Teaching Torah* and *Teaching Haftarah* (A.R.E./Behrman House). If the portion is not immediately relevant to children because it does not feature a story, consider a theme from the portion or an upcoming holiday. For example, when reading the detailed sections about the construction of the Tabernacle, talk about the importance of making things we love beautiful. You can read from the Torah directly, or read a book on a connected theme (or about an upcoming holiday). If you are reading from the Torah itself, practice in advance in order to model for children *kavod laTorah* (respect for the Torah). This is also a good time to invite clergy into the service to speak with the children or to tell a Torah story.

Taking the Torah Out of the Ark

The choreography of the Torah service mirrors the giving of the Torah at Mount Sinai. Traditionally, first an individual is honored with opening the ark. Another person holds the Torah and sings *Sh'ma Yisrael*, to which the congregation responds by repeating the same words aloud. Congregants then parade the Torah around the congregation; as the Torah passes by, many congregants reach out to touch it with the corner of a tallit or siddur, which they may then kiss. The Torah is brought to a reading table, where its cover is removed, and it is opened. Traditionally, a person known as the *gabbai* is responsible for calling people up to the Torah and maintaining the flow of the service.

Having an Aliyah

The honor of coming to the Torah to say the blessings before and after the reading is called an *aliyah*. Traditionally, only Jewish adults over age 13 are invited for an *aliyah*, but in family services, children are often given *aliyot* in order to practice reciting the blessing. Provide a copy of these blessings with transliteration at the reading table. A different person—trained in Torah reading—is usually responsible for actually reading from the Torah. Traditionally, the *gabbai* calls the individual honored with an *aliyah* to the Torah by saying *Ta'amod* (followed by their name in Hebrew or English) in the case of a female, *Ya'amod* in the case of a male, and *Ya'amdu* in the case of a couple or family. Before saying the blessing, the Torah reader shows the honoree where the reading will begin, usually with a *yad* (pointer). The honoree, using a corner of a tallit, the Torah "belt," or a siddur touches that spot and then kisses the tallit, Torah belt, or siddur. The honoree then recites the blessing on page 36.

The Torah reader then begins reading. When the reading is complete, the *aliyah* honoree touches the last word read with the corner of the tallit, Torah belt, or siddur, and kisses it. He or she then recites the blessing on page 37. When an *aliyah* is complete, the honoree moves to the other side of the reading table until the next *aliyah* is complete. We congratulate the honoree with the colloquial phrase *yasher ko'ach* ("strength be with you" or "good job!"). While traditionally there are seven *aliyot* on Shabbat morning, in family services consider giving just three *aliyot* in order to hold everyone's attention.

Putting the Torah Away

After the Torah reader has completed the reading, a participant has the honor of lifting the Torah so that the entire group can see its columns (this is called *hagbahah*), while V'zot HaTorah (at the top of page 38) is sung, and then the Torah is tightly rolled and dressed (an honor called *g'lilah*). The Torah is then paraded around the congregation for a second time and placed back in the Ark as the community sings Eitz Chayim Hi – "[The Torah] is a tree of life" (page 38).

Incorporating Art

- We call the Torah a "tree of life," as depicted in the art in *Siddur Mah Tov*. Ask: What do a tree and the Torah have in common? (*strong roots, a wide reach*) To what else would you compare the Torah?

Incorporating Movement

- After carrying the Torah around to the congregation, sing a song that relates to the weekly portion or to an upcoming Jewish holiday. For example, when reading a *parashah* about the building of the Tabernacle, sing "If I Had a Hammer." [xi]
- Though traditionally one or two people at a time are given an *aliyah*, you may stage a collective *aliyah* for all the children.[xii]
- Invite children and parents with upcoming birthdays to come to the Torah for a special *aliyah* and birthday blessing.
- Invite people to come for *aliyot* based on the theme of the portion of the Torah you read. For example, if reading the story of Noah, invite people who love animals to come to the Torah for an *aliyah*.

- After the *aliyot*, offer a Mi Shebeirach (prayer for healing) for those who are ill. This is an opportunity for adults and children alike to offer the names of people they love who are in need of healing.[xiii]
- After you read a section of the Torah in Hebrew, immediately translate it into simple English. If you desire, the English translator can be a different person from the Hebrew reader.

Incorporating Discussion/Narrative
- In our prayer service, we talk to God. When we read the Torah, it is as if God is talking to us through its messages and stories (Rabbi Louis Finkelstein, a twentieth-century scholar). Invite participants to listen carefully to today's Torah passage. What message do they find?
- Invite individual families to meet with the clergy to prepare a *d'var Torah* for presentation in the family service sometime during the year. Each family studies the *parashah*. Then families prepare a discussion, skit, song, or art to present on their designated week.[xiv]

Incorporating Props
- Use a tallit or create a *chupah* decorated by the families of the community, under which the children gather to hear a Torah story.[xv]
- While reading from the Torah, roll it out on families' knees (put *tallitot* over their knees first), or hold it upright as Sephardic communities do.
- Before the service begins, each participant receives a card containing the name of one leadership role in the Torah service (*open the ark, take Torah out of the ark, gabbai, aliyah, hagbahah, g'lilah, put the Torah back*) and instructions for how to fulfill that role. This activity teaches participants how to have an *aliyah* and become more familiar with Torah service choreography.[xvi]
- Demonstrate *hagbahah* and *g'lilah*, lifting and dressing the Torah after the reading. Explain the reasons that we lift the scroll (*so everyone can see the words and feel as if they are a part of the reading, to give honor to the Torah*), and give each willing and able person a chance to lift it. This will help participants feel confident with this honor during synagogue services.[xvii]
- Everyone has roles in the Torah service, even if they do not come to the Torah reading table. Teach participants to respond correctly when the Torah blessings are recited and also how to say the customary phrase of congratulations, *yasher ko'ach*, to someone who has received an honor.[xviii]
- Baby Naming Service. Children are invited to bring their "babies" (stuffed animals, dolls) to a special Torah service. On the day of the service, the leader speaks with the children about the importance of names and the Jewish ritual of baby naming. The children go up for *aliyot* in groups with their babies. The children then receive a blessing that links the joy of naming their babies to the joys of Judaism, Shabbat, and celebrating as a community. Give each participant a certificate of naming. End the program with a *kiddush* replete with doll tea sets and small chairs for the babies.[xix]

Aleinu
Page 40
Aleinu says that it is our responsibility to recognize God's presence in the world and implies that we should work as God's partner to create a better world. We stand while reciting the Aleinu.

Incorporating Movement
- During the Aleinu, we bow to acknowledge God's presence in the world. At *va'anachnu kor'im*, we bend our knees, bow at *u'mishtachavim*, and straighten at *lifnei Melech*.

Incorporating Discussion/Narrative
- We acknowledge in the Aleinu that we are proud to be Jewish. Ask participants: What makes you proud to be Jewish? How do you show that you are proud to be Jewish?

Mourner's Kaddish
Page 42

Mourners recite the Kaddish after the death of a loved one, as well as on the anniversary of the death. The Mourner's Kaddish, traditionally recited in the presence of a minyan, does not mention death; rather, it praises God. It is written in Aramaic, the language Jews spoke in Israel in the Second Temple period (516 BCE – 70 CE) and after. Though some adults may be uncomfortable discussing death with children, exposing them to the Kaddish teaches children about our responsibility to support people who have suffered a loss. It also teaches children basic Jewish literacy, so that when the time comes that they might need to recite the Kaddish themselves, they are comfortable with the words and the rhythm of the prayer. In some communities, mourners and those observing a *yahrtzeit* (the anniversary of a death) are the only ones who stand during the Mourner's Kaddish. In other communities, everyone rises.

Incorporating Art
- *Siddur Mah Tov* depicts the Mourner's Kaddish with a single candle in the darkness. Mourners light a memorial candle when a loved one dies. Ask participants: Why is the candle an important symbol? (*a flickering candle in the darkness reminds us of the fragility of life*)

Incorporating Discussion/Narrative
- Ask: In the Mourner's Kaddish, we remember people we love who are no longer living. Whom do you remember today?

Adon Olam
Page 44

Adon Olam closes the service by attesting to God's everlasting presence in the world. Its rhythmic, singable quality invites many different tunes, thus allowing you to end the service on an upbeat and creative note.

Incorporating Art
- Ask: The image of the world in *Siddur Mah Tov* reminds us that though we are praying in synagogue, our prayers and actions can impact the world around us. In what ways do you think this is true?

Incorporating Discussion/Narrative
- Assign families different weeks to lead Adon Olam. Challenge families to find and bring new tunes for Adon Olam. An Internet search will easily bring up a variety of tunes. Ask: Which tune for Adon Olam is your favorite, and how does it make you feel?

Incorporating Props
- In communities that use instruments on Shabbat, children can receive various instruments, including flutes, trumpets, triangles, bells, and cymbals, to make an Adon Olam Band. Children receive instructions to play their own instruments at specific points in the song. Other children take turns using a large pointer and a poster with text to aid everyone in following along in Hebrew. In communities that do not use instruments on Shabbat, children may pantomime playing instruments. Encourage all children to sing loudly.

Kiddush and Hamotzi
> Page 46

Kiddush is a highlight of all services, especially family services. The act of eating together can be very powerful, and the words and tunes of Kiddush and Hamotzi are powerful, too. The words of the Kiddush, from the book of Exodus, remind us of the act of Creation and the unique nature of Shabbat. Both Kiddush and Hamotzi remind us to be thankful for all that we eat and our partnership with God in creating food.

Incorporating Art
- You don't need a *picture* of the challah and grape juice (or wine) to remind you to eat. Create a warm *kiddush* atmosphere with an actual challah and grape juice. You can add cookies, crackers, fruit, and other special treats for a sweet ending.

Incorporating Movement
- Create hand signals illustrating the words of Kiddush and Hamotzi.

Incorporating Discussion/Narrative
- After we recite Kiddush and Hamotzi we eat and play together, which is an important way for us to create community. What can you do to make others feel welcome at *kiddush*? (*introduce yourself, bring treats to share, share toys*)

Incorporating Props
- Consider giving young children a wooden or plastic Kiddush cup and toy challah over which to say the *b'rachot* and then distribute real food separately.

How to Make the Most Out of Kiddush
- Have a volunteer make announcements.
- Have a volunteer pre-pour Kiddush grape juice and cut the challah while you sing Adon Olam.
- Encourage participants to reintroduce themselves after Hamotzi.
- Once a month celebrate birthdays with cupcakes.
- Read a Jewish story after *kiddush*.
- Collect age-appropriate toys and games for children to play with during and after *kiddush*.

Troubleshooting
The following techniques will help you respond appropriately when you encounter troublesome issues in your family services.

There are discipline problems, such as children behaving disrespectfully:
- Set the expectation at the beginning of services that all participants behave with *derech eretz*—proper behavior and respect for others. If necessary, discuss as a group the meaning of *derech eretz*.
- In the case of an individual child, be direct and talk to the parent in private about what you and they can do to improve the behavior.
- Ask a trusted parent or staff member to observe the service and reflect afterward with you. Make sure the observer notes in particular the following common pitfalls: the use of transitions, the presentation of questions, room setup.

Parents are talking constantly during the service:
- Privately, ask those parents to help you model good synagogue behavior.
- The parents may not be engaged in the service. Determine how you can engage them further, for example, by requesting their leadership or by offering more high-level discussion.
- Parents' poor behavior may reflect their sense that they are not needed and that their children can attend services on their own. Depending on the age of the child and the style of the service, perhaps the child can be left alone in the service while the parent attends adult services.

People don't know the words and/or the melodies:
- Don't panic if families don't know all of the words or the tunes; repetition is key. Encourage families to hum or clap along. If you use the same tunes for a while, the "regulars" will pick up on them and will support you.
- Teach a core parent group the words and tunes before the service so they know them in advance. Provide them with a CD or MP3 downloads on your synagogue Web site.
- Create posterboard displays with core prayer words on them.
- Use *Siddur Mah Tov* and encourage families to follow along however feels best to them: in Hebrew, transliteration, translation, or illustration.
- Remember that it doesn't matter how well you sing—your passion and energy are most important. However, if your community values musicality, then the service leader should be someone who is musical and reflects that value.

I've never used props before:
- Leadership and teaching require experimentation. Playing with props can enliven a service. Try a few and see how they feel. For example, use instruments, puppets, or posters.
- Some leaders have great success using puppets. Others aren't puppet people. If you'd like to try it, do it! For example, you can use a puppet when telling a story during the Torah service. Try three times before determining whether it works for you.

I've prepared for 3rd graders but only kindergartners show up:
- Teach to the oldest kids in the room so that they do not feel that they are in a "baby service."
- Remind participants about the age group for which the service is designed. If the attendance of many younger siblings changes the intended demographic, speak with parents and synagogue professionals to determine whether to restructure the age group of the service.

I want to get teens involved:
- Invite post-bar and bat mitzvah teens, who can otherwise be difficult to engage, to assist in leading the service.
- Invite teens in to present a play or act out a scene from the Torah portion.

Appendix

Suggested Outline of the Shabbat Morning Service for Tots (3 and Younger)

SECTION	PRAYERS AND SONGS	PAGE IN *SIDDUR MAH TOV*
Warm-Up Birchot Hashachar	"Bim Bam/Shabbat Shalom"	
	Modeh/Modah Ani	4
	Mah Tovu	6
	Birchot Hashachar Recommended: • *Asher natan lasechvi* • *Pokei'ach ivrim* • *Malbish arumim*	8
Halleluyah	Psalm 150	10
	V'nomar Lefanav (Conservative) Hal'lu-Hodu LaShem (Conservative)	12 (C) 12 (C)
Sh'ma	Sh'ma	20 (R), 22 (C)
	Mi Chamochah	26
Amidah	Private moment with parent	28
Torah Service	Plush Torah parade	
	"Torah, Torah, Torah"	
	Torah story or song	
	Eitz Chayim Hi	38
Concluding Prayers	Oseh Shalom	32
	Adon Olam	44
Kiddush	Kiddush	46
	Hamotzi	46

Suggested Outline of the Shabbat Morning Service for Children Ages 4–8

SECTION	PRAYERS AND SONGS	PAGE IN SIDDUR MAH TOV
Warm-Up Birchot Hashachar	"Bim Bam/Shabbat Shalom"	
	Putting on the tallit (if it is the custom in your synagogue)	
	Modeh/Modah Ani	4
	Mah Tovu	6
	Hinei Mah-Tov	6
	Birchot Hashachar (select)	8
Halleluyah	Psalm 150 (with percussion)	10
	V'nomar Lefanav (Conservative)	12 (C)
	Hal'lu-Hodu LaShem (Conservative)	12 (C)
Bar'chu	Bar'chu	12 (R), 14 (C)
	Ahavah Rabah	16 (R), 18 (C)
Sh'ma	Sh'ma with traditional tune or hand signals	20 (R), 22 (C)
	V'ahavta	22 (R), 24 (C)
	Mi Chamochah	26
Amidah	Adonai S'fatai Tiftach	28
	Amidah	28
	K'dushah	31
	Silent Prayer	32
	Oseh Shalom	32
Torah Service	Taking out the Torah	34
	Circulating with the Torah	
	Torah Reading	36
	Telling the Torah story	
	Putting Away the Torah	38
	Eitz Chayim Hi	38
Concluding Prayers	Aleinu	40
	Mourner's Kaddish	42
	Adon Olam	44
Kiddush	Kiddush	46
	Hamotzi	46
	Announcements	

The most logical place to insert other songs (see partial list below) is at the beginning of the service or during the Torah service.

Other songs:
"David Melech Yisrael"
"Shalom Chaverim"
"Am Yisrael Chai"
"The Shabbat Pokey" (like "The Hokey Pokey" but with Hebrew designations for body parts)
"Hinei Rakevet"
"Mah Yafeh Hayom"
"If You're Happy and You Know It" (Kiss/Hug/Lift Your Torah)
"Achshav, Achshav B'Eretz Yisrael"
"Zum Gali Gali"

---

[i] Janette Silverman, Beth El Congregation, Phoenix, AZ
[ii] Rabbi Rebecca Rosenthal, Congregation B'nai Zion, El Paso, TX
[iii] Osnat Kalati, Temple Beth Ahm Yisrael, Springfield, NJ
[iv] Osnat Kalati, Temple Beth Ahm Yisrael, Springfield, NJ
[v] Rabbi Nicki Greninger, Temple Isaiah, Lafayette, CA
[vi] Selma Roffman, Kellman Brown Academy, Voorhees, NJ
[vii] Cantor Steve Abramowitz, Temple Beth Torah, Holliston, MA
[viii] Cantor Steve Abramowitz, Temple Beth Torah, Holliston, MA
[ix] Rabbi Randy Kafka, Temple Israel South Shore, North Easton, MA
[x] Rabbi Jeffrey Goldwasser, Congregation Beth Israel, North Adams, MA
[xi] Rabbi Rachel Ain, Congregation Beth Sholom-Chevra Shas, Jamesville, NY
[xii] Rabbi Rachel Ain, Congregation Beth Sholom-Chevra Shas, Jamesville, NY
[xiii] Rabbi Rachel Ain, Congregation Beth Sholom-Chevra Shas, Jamesville, NY
[xiv] Rabbi Jeni S. Friedman, Temple Beth Sholom, Roslyn Heights, NY
[xv] Niema Hirsch, Congregation Beth El, Fairfield, CT
[xvi] Sharon B. Wasserberg, Adath Israel Congregation, Cincinnati, OH
[xvii] Valerie Lieber, Kane Street Synagogue, Brooklyn, NY
[xviii] Valerie Lieber, Kane Street Synagogue, Brooklyn, NY
[xix] Debrah Gladstone, Temple Beth Am, Randolph, MA

Notes